JARS OF HOPE

by **Jennifer Roy**
illustrated by **Meg Owenson**

HOW ONE WOMAN HELPED SAVE 2,500 CHILDREN DURING THE HOLOCAUST

Content Consultant: Mary Skinner, 2B Productions
Director and Producer of the PBS documentary
Irena Sendler: In the Name of Their Mothers

CAPSTONE PRESS

OTWOCK, POLAND, 1917

Irena noticed things.

She noticed that some people were treated differently than others. Sometimes Irena's father took her with him on his doctor's visits. The children in the neighborhood where he treated patients spoke Yiddish. They also went to the Jewish temple.

Irena heard the mean things that others said about the Jewish people. Most people in her neighborhood stayed away from the Jewish neighborhoods. Irena often played with the Jewish children.

"Papa," Irena asked, "Are some people really better than others?"

"Irena," her beloved father said, "There are two kinds of people in this world, good and bad. It doesn't matter if they are rich or poor, what religion or race. What matters is if they are good or bad."

Irena's father died when she was only 7 years old. But his wise words did not die with him. They lived on In Irena's heart.

WARSAW, POLAND, 1940

Irena wanted to be a good person.

To help poor families in Warsaw, she took a job as a social worker.

In 1939 Germany had invaded Poland. Germany's leader, Adolf Hitler, led the Nazi Party. He believed Jewish people were unequal to the Germans. World War II had begun.

"I'm here to give people vaccines," said Irena. She was entering the Warsaw Ghetto. By 1940 Germans had forced almost 500,000 Polish Jews to move into this space within the city. It was less than 2 square miles (5.2 square kilometers). A tall brick wall topped with barbed wire and shards of glass surrounded the ghetto. The Germans had told the Polish people a lie—they were not allowed to enter the ghetto because they'd catch diseases.

"Go in," said the soldier. "We don't want sickness spreading outside these walls."

Irena was frightened at first, but she had seen how badly the Nazis treated the Jews. She was worried about all of the people trapped in the ghetto simply because of their religion.

"Miss, do you have any food?" a child called to Irena.

"My baby is sick," a woman pleaded. "Please, can you help?"

"There are so many people in need," thought Irena.
"What can one person do?"

Irena thought of something her father had told her. "When someone is drowning," he had said, "give him your hand."

"The children are hurting the most," she decided.
"I have to give them a helping hand."

Irena talked to friends she could trust.

"We can sneak food and medicine into the ghetto,"
Irena told them, "if we are very careful."

"It will be dangerous," said her friend Jaga Piotrowska.
"If the Nazis catch us, they may kill us."

"So, will you do it?" Irena asked.

"Of course," Jaga responded.

Irena and her helpers bravely began sneaking food,
medicine, and other aid into the ghetto. But soon their
mission became more urgent … and even more dangerous.

Starting in July 1942, German soldiers forced more than 6,000 Jewish people per day into cattle cars on trains. The Jews had no idea where they were going. The trains took them to Treblinka, a place where the Nazis would put them to death.

Irena organized.

Irena had many helpers. One was a truck driver named Antoni. He was allowed to drive the truck in and out of the ghetto. The first time he and Irena tried to sneak out a baby in the truck, the baby cried. The German soldiers at the gate almost caught them.

The next time Irena brought a child to the truck, she found a surprise. There was a large dog in the front seat!

"This is Shepsi," Antoni said. "She's quite talented and is well trained. We don't need to worry about the baby in the back crying," he whispered.

The truck inched its way to the border gate and stopped.
From the back, the baby began to wail. The guard came closer.

"Oh, no!" thought Irena. "Surely we will be caught!"

Just then Antoni tapped Shepsi's paw. The big dog began barking, which
made the soldier's dogs bark too. The loud dogs drowned out the
baby's cries, and the guard let the truck pass through the ghetto gates.

JULY 18, 1942

Irena knocked on a door.

When the door opened, she took a deep breath and walked in. "It is time," she said.

Henia Koppel gently placed her baby girl into Irena's carpenter's toolbox. Irena looked down at baby Bieta—her innocent face, her tiny body snuggled into the blanket she was wrapped in. The baby smiled. Irena put a dropper of medicine into Bieta's mouth to make her sleepy. She fixed the blanket, making sure the box's air holes were clear.

As Irena began to close the box, the baby's grandfather quickly slipped something inside. It was a small silver spoon marked with the baby's name and birthday: *Elzbieta, 5 January 1942.*

"A gift from her Momma and Poppa," he said, wiping tears from his eyes.

Irena took a deep breath. She stepped out into the Warsaw Ghetto, carrying her precious cargo.

Irena knocked on more doors.

"Please let your child go with me," Irena begged. "I will do my best to save him."

"What promise can you give us that our child will live?" the parents asked Irena.

"I can only guarantee that if your child stays here, he will die," Irena answered.

When the parents agreed to let their child go, Irena had to make a decision. What was the best way to rescue this child?

"Your child is small," Irena told the parents of the youngest ones. "We will smuggle her out …

inside a potato sack, hidden in a coffin,

or underneath the trash in a cart."

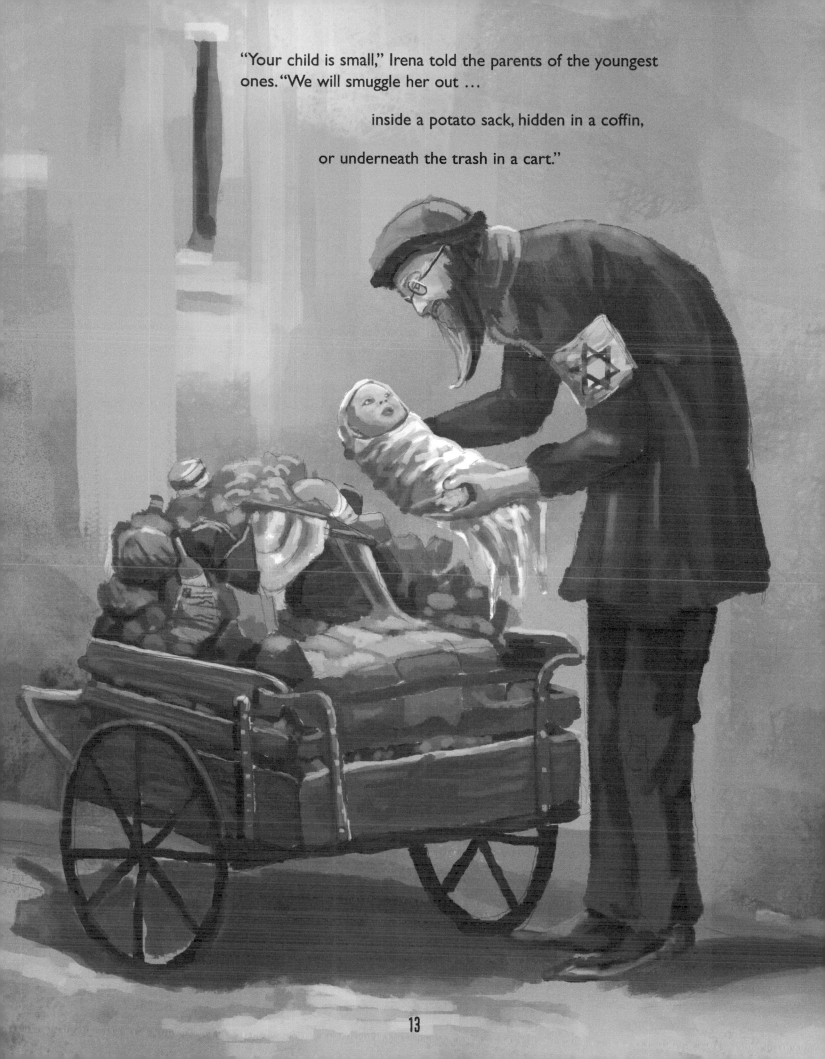

Irena spoke directly to the older children she rescued.

"Be brave," she said. "From this moment, your name is not Isaac.
It is Piotr. Say your new name over and over, until you believe you
are Piotr. Then you must quickly memorize the Lord's Prayer. You are
now a Catholic child."

Piotr learned and practiced the Lord's Prayer, making the sign of the cross
as he spoke it.

"Good," said Irena. "Now you are ready. Follow me."

They hurried into the courthouse that straddled the border of the ghetto.
Irena made Piotr change out of his old clothes and into new, fresh ones.
Then they walked through the back door, which led outside the ghetto to safety.

Other times Irena's helpers were busy underground.
The helpers, called liaisons, led the Jewish children through
the maze of sewer tunnels to freedom and safety.

NOVEMBER, 1942

Irena joined Zegota.

Zegota was a secret group of brave Polish men and women that wanted to aid and rescue Jews. Irena would be in charge of helping the Jewish children. She and her network continued sneaking children out of the ghetto every day. But where did the children go?

Irena found many brave people to take in the children. There were foster families who agreed to keep the smaller children. Some children went to Polish orphanages. Others went to convents, where nuns took care of them.

Everyone knew that if they were caught hiding a Jewish child, they would be put to death. But these courageous people risked their own lives to save the children. They knew it was the right thing to do.

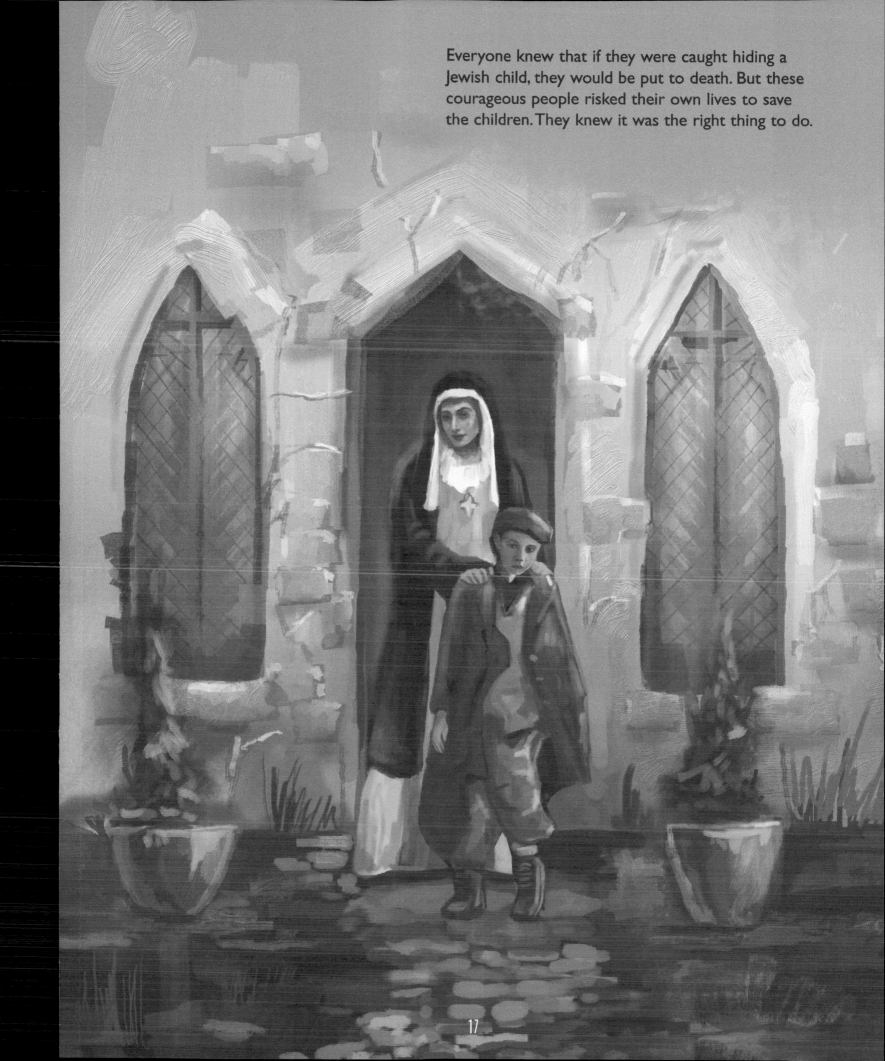

Irena kept records.

Not only did Irena and her helpers rescue children, they made sure each child was safe and well cared for. Irena and her helpers delivered money, supplies, and food to the foster families who cared for the children.

"The children are in good hands now," Irena told her friend Jaga. "But when the war ends, they will need to be reunited with their parents. I have been keeping lists of the children's real names, along with their new names and where they are."

"Me too," said Jaga. "If the Nazis find the lists, they may kill us and hunt down the children and their caregivers."

"Every child deserves to know her real name," Irena insisted. "And the children's families will want to find them. But you're right—it is very dangerous, and we need to be careful."

IRENA'S APARTMENT, OCTOBER 20, 1943

Irena was caught.

She always knew that saving children came with great risk. Her greatest fear was about to become very real.

Bang! Bang! Bang!

"Open up!" a man shouted, pounding on the door.

"It's the Gestapo!" Irena whispered.

Irena grabbed her lists and went to the window to throw them outside. But there were more secret police waiting out there! The building was surrounded!

Bang! Bang!

Irena desperately tossed the list of names to Janina, a friend who was staying with her. Janina stuck the lists under her arm, beneath her clothing. Then Irena opened the door.

Gestapo police swarmed into the room. They tore apart Irena's home, but they did not find the lists.

They did, however, take Irena away.

PAWIAK PRISON, OCTOBER 1943

Irena went to prison.

Pawiak Prison was a place where the Gestapo questioned and punished anyone who broke Nazi law.

"Tell us what you know about Zegota," the Gestapo policeman demanded.

"I don't know anything," Irena replied. "I'm just a social worker."

The man lashed Irena's legs and feet, first with a whip, then with a strap.

But Irena stayed silent.

Irena's days were always the same.

In prison Irena worked 12 hours a day scrubbing laundry. Then she was questioned and beaten for not giving up the names of her Zegota friends. She got very little food. Hunger and pain kept her from getting a good night's sleep. Days turned into months—3 months.

PAWIAK PRISON, JANUARY 1944

Irena's name was called.

"Irena Sendler!" a guard yelled.

Irena was pushed into a truck with other women crammed inside.
They were taken to Gestapo headquarters.

"We will be put to death," Irena thought. "I am proud I did not give
up any information. I am not afraid to die."

Irena was pushed into a room and fell on her knees.
An officer pulled her up and led her through a door.

"You are free," the officer said in Polish. "Get out of here
as fast as you can."

Irena limped and stumbled on her damaged legs
and feet down an alleyway. The sun came out
from behind a cloud. Irena was blinded for
a moment. She had not seen the sun
for 100 days.

Irena hid.

Zegota had paid the officer a lot of money to free Irena. But now she had to go into hiding because the Nazis believed she was dead.

Irena hid in friends' houses. For a few days, she even hid in the Warsaw Zoo, sleeping in a cage with baby foxes. But she continued her work with Zegota, and thanks to her friend, she still had the lists of children she had saved.

LATE SUMMER, 1944

Irena hid the lists.

The Warsaw Uprising had begun. There was fighting in the streets. Irena wanted to make sure her lists would be safe, even if something happened to her.

At midnight one night, she and Jaga tiptoed outside Jaga's house to the backyard. The friends dug into the hard ground with a knife and spoon. Irena lowered three jars into the hole and covered them with soil. The lists were safe. Jars of names. Jars of hope.

AFTERWORD

After the war's end, Irena's lists were given to an organization that was helping connect survivors with their families. Sadly, most of the children's parents had died. But a few were alive and were able to find their children because of Irena's lists.

Some children learned of their real history and their parents' brave decision to give them up to save their lives. And still others remembered Irena herself, courageous and comforting, leading them to freedom.

Years later people would ask, "Irena, why did you do it? Why did you risk your life to save Jewish children?"

"Under German occupation," Irena responded, "I saw the Polish nation drowning, and those in the most difficult position were the Jews. And those who needed the most help were the children. So I had to help."

On May 12, 2008, Irena was eating breakfast with her friend Bieta. It was the same Bieta who, as a baby, was carried out of the ghetto in a toolbox. The grown up Bieta had lost her parents in the war, but she still had the spoon to remember them by. Irena, now age 98, was in a good mood and the two friends chatted. Irena closed her eyes and peacefully died.

Irena Sendler was honored by Yad Vashem, the Jewish people's living memorial to the Holocaust in Israel. She was presented with a medal inscribed with the words,

"Whosoever saves a single life, saves an entire universe."

Irena never thought of herself as a hero.

"Let me first say that I had many helpers," Irena said. "The world should never forget them. It is not true that this was a heroic act, only a simple and natural need of the heart."

AUTHOR'S NOTE

In 1999 a ninth grade student from Uniontown, Kansas, read a newspaper article about a Polish woman named Irena Sendler. Irena had saved more than 2,500 children from the Nazis.

"How come I've never heard of her before?" Elizabeth wondered.

She asked around. No one knew about Irena Sendler. With the help of her teacher, Mr. Conard, Elizabeth and two other students, Megan Stewart and Sabrina Coons, wrote and performed a short play about Irena's heroic acts.

Elizabeth, Megan, and Sabrina won prizes for their play. More students joined the original girls to perform the play and tell Irena's story.

Elizabeth, Megan, and Sabrina also flew to Poland and met Irena Sendler. Although she was now elderly, she still had a twinkle in her eyes and the same love of children.

Irena was living proof that the Holocaust was not just something you'd read in a history book. It was real, and it happened to real people.

Like my Aunt Sylvia.

"How did no one ever hear about this?" I thought, stunned, as my aunt told the story of her childhood in the Lodz Ghetto in Lodz, Poland. Like the girls in Kansas, I wanted to share the incredible story. So I wrote the book, *Yellow Star*.

Little Syvia (who grew up to be my Aunt Sylvia) was in a ghetto only 80 miles away from Irena Sendler. Although their stories are very different, they both kept something special in their hearts, even in the darkest times.

Hope.

Jennifer Roy

August 12, 2014

GLOSSARY

cargo—goods carried

convent—a building where a group of religious women live

foster home—a safe place where children can live for a short time; social workers find foster homes for some children

Gestapo—the secret police of Nazi Germany

Holocaust—during World War II, the mass murder of millions of Jews, as well as gypsies, disabled people, homosexuals, and political and religious leaders

Jewish—describing Judaism, a religion based on a belief in one God and the teachings of a holy book called the Torah

Nazi—a member of a political party led by Adolf Hitler; the Nazis ruled Germany from 1933 to 1945

orphanage—a place that provides a home for children whose parents have died or are absent

uprising—a revolt, usually against a government

vaccine—a medicine that prevents a disease

World War II—a war in which the United States, France, Great Britain, the Soviet Union and other countries defeated Germany, Italy, and Japan; World War II lasted from 1939 to 1945

Yiddish—a language used by Jews in central and eastern Europe before the Holocaust; today it is spoken by some people in the United States, Israel, and Russia

Zegota—a secret group of Polish men and women who worked together to aid the Jews in Poland during World War II

INDEX

SOURCE NOTES

Page 3, line 3: Jack Mayer. *Life in a Jar: The Irena Sendler Project.* Middlebury, Vt.: Long Trail Press, 2011, p. 88.

Page 5, line 5: Mary Skinner, dir. and prod. *Irena Sendler: In the Name of Their Mothers.* PBS, 2011. Film.

Page 28, line 10: Jack Mayer. *Life in a Jar: The Irena Sendler Project.* Middlebury, Vt.: Long Trail Press, 2011, p. 313–314.

Page 28, line 23: Jack Mayer. *Life in a Jar: The Irena Sendler Project.* Middlebury, Vt.: Long Trail Press, 2011, p. 310 and 314.

Author Bio

Jennifer Roy is the author of the modern classic *Yellow Star*, the true story of her aunt's survival during the Holocaust; the award-winning *Mindblind* about a teen with Asperger's Syndrome; and the best-selling *Trading Faces* series coauthored with her twin sister, Julie DeVillers. Jennifer and her family currently reside in Saratoga Springs, New York.

Illustrator Bio

Meg Owenson is a talented Illustrator and Concept Artist working from her small seaside studio in Scarborough, UK. Since graduating with a degree in Fine Art, she has worked on everything from computer games and film to books and apparel.

Thanks to our adviser for her expertise, research, and advice:
Mary Skinner, 2B Productions
Director and Producer of the PBS documentary about Irena Sendler
Irena Sendler: In the Name of Their Mothers

Editor: Shelly Lyons
Designer: Ashlee Suker
Creative Director: Nathan Gassman
Production Specialist: Tori Abraham
The illustrations in this book were created digitally and traditionally drawn.

Published by Capstone Press,
1710 Roe Crest Drive, North Mankato, Minnesota 56003
www.mycapstone.com

Library of Congress Cataloging-in-Publication Data
Roy, Jennifer, author.
Jars of hope : how one woman helped save 2,500 children during the Holocaust / by Jennifer Roy.
pages cm — (Encounter)
Includes bibliographical references and index.
Summary: "Tells Irena Sendler's story of saving 2,500 children during the Holocaust"— Provided by publisher.
ISBN 978-1-4914-6072-6 (library binding)
ISBN 978-1-4914-6553-0 (paperback)
ISBN 978-1-62370-425-4 (paper over board)
ISBN 978-1-4914-6554-7 (eBook PDF)
1. Sendlerowa, Irena, 1910-2008—Juvenile literature. 2. Righteous Gentiles in the Holocaust—Poland—Biography—Juvenile literature. 3. Jewish children in the Holocaust—Poland—Warsaw—Juvenile literature. 4. World War 1939-1945—Jews—Rescue—Poland—Juvenile literature. 5. World War, 1939-1945—Poland—Warsaw—Juvenile literature. 6. Holocaust, Jewish (1939-1945)—Poland—Juvenile literature. 7. Poland—Ethnic relations—History—20th century—Juvenile literature. I. Title.
  D804.66.S46R69 2015
  940.53'18092—dc23 [B]   2014049602

Printed in the United States   5038